Welcome, Dangerous Life

Welcome, Dangerous Life

Poems by Ben Gunsberg

Turning Point

Published by Turning Point
P.O. Box 541106
Cincinnati, OH 45254-1106

ISBN: 9781625492876

Poetry Editor: Kevin Walzer
Business Editor: Lori Jareo

Cover art by Joan Andrea Merrell, "As Day and Night are One."

Visit us on the web at www.turningpointbooks.com

ACKNOWLEDGEMENTS

Grateful acknowledgement is made to the editors of the following journals, who first published versions of these poems.

A Bad Penny Review: "Machine Overheard Teaching Boy to Read"

The Broken Plate: "Body Art"

Cactus Heart: "Self-Portrait as Mole at the End of the World"

The Cape Rock: "Closed KFC"

Chariton Review: "Swamp," "Prodigal Self," and "Tagged"

Chattahoochee Review: "Trapped American Goldfinch" and "Scout"

Cold Mountain Review: "Pando"

Common Ground Review: "One Lousy Enemy" and "Welcome, Dangerous Life"

CutBank: "Incredible Shrinking Man"

DoveTales: "Audubon Exit" and "What to Do with Minnesota"

Great Lakes Review: "Ann Arbor"

Gris-Gris: "Breakfall"

The Houston Poetry Festival 2015 Anthology: "Hoedown for Dualists"

JuxtaProse Literary Magazine: "No Emergency" and "The Heroic Age"

JMWW: "Interview" and "Vernice Bianca"

Mid-American Review: "Floating Exhibit"

Naugatuck River Review: "What Fernando Saw"

Off the Coast: "Rhapsody for Real Estate"

Pacific Review: "Inversions"

Painted Bride Quarterly: "Forgiving Indianapolis"

Permafrost: "Husband, Mugged"

Pilgrimage: "Black Jack Peers Over the Bed"

Prompt Press: "Twin Days"

The Santa Ana River Review: "At the Window"

South Carolina Review: "Breaking Bread"

Stirring: "Night Terrors" and "Morals from *The Treasury of Pleasure Books for Young Children*"

Sugar House Review: "Athena" and "Reseeding a Nature Trope"

The Red Mountain Review: "We Played Them Fast and Made Mistakes"

The Southeast Review: "Burning the Nest"

The Sow's Ear Poetry Review: "Narcissus and Narcissus"

Tupelo Quarterly Review: "Rhapsody for Children of the Midwest"

Valparaiso Poetry Review: "Escape from Heroic Music"

Works and Days Quarterly: "Thanatos and Eros"

The following poems also appeared in the chapbook *Rhapsodies with Portraits* (Finishing Line Press, 2015): "Rhapsody for Children of the Midwest," "Self-Portrait with Silly Putty," "One Lousy Enemy," "Portrait of Utility," "Forgiving Indianapolis," "Trapped American Goldfinch," "Welcome, Dangerous Life," "Rhapsody for Real Estate," "Husband, Mugged," "Failed Still Life with Jealousy," "Self-Portrait with Lopper," "What Fernando Saw," "Self-Portrait as a Mole at the End of the World."

For Andrea, Maya, and Isaac

CONTENTS

I. Lost & Found

II. Love Debt

III. Restless Animal

IV. Less-than-perfect chain

I. Lost & Found

No Storm

Could be a young John Glenn
who gazes at the moon as it breaks
the barrier of a cloud and forgets
the dangers of space travel, absolutely
no sensation of the increasing speed
with which a body falls toward the Atlantic.

Or a Cousteau who bears the same
proportion of water as the surface of the earth
and returns to sea, happy to drift
with lantern fish and bronze eels,
unclipped from cables, sheathed
by helmeted suit and languid flippers.

He sits beneath a solitary palm,
waits for wind to ripple the surface,
for rain to stage a drummers' revolution,
every viridescent frond, every wood ring
poised for renovation.
                              He makes repairs,
scrubs the transom.
Time to lie on a sun-soaked deck

while a jet leaves its powdery trace

against the sky. The drinking water

has not run dry. He helps himself

to pickles and molasses.

Rhapsody for Children of the Midwest

What a blast! Crossing the community yard,
ketchup on our lips, chocolate milk fresh as a hiccup,
Illinois sky scrubbed peasant white, our eyes
flecked with pollen. Erik, Alan, Nina, Mike,
race me to a public pool, where sun shatters
like a chandelier and lifeguards punch our ears
with whistles. Let's ride our bikes to Missouri,
where rivers sluice like turkey gravy.
O brown lament, O mosquito, O inner tube
slick as a hippo. Erik, Alan, Nina, Mike,
float with me into the swamp-thick heart
of Cape Girardeau while Baptist churches break
into song. Just passing through this picnic,
this Boy Scout troop, this Vacation Bible School,
sampling potato salad and Christ's gold corona,
praying our fathers land better jobs up north
in Michigan, where bass and trout sleep in
deeper lakes and December plasters shore,
for it's damn cold today as we don skates,
click across the ice, arms like metronomes
set at different speeds, the lake's shimmering
scalp beneath our blades, a half-circle of spruce,

a lone snowman engrossed, his future secured
by flakes that share his ontology, which we catch
on our tongues. Snow forgives the ruins of Detroit,
smothers ragweed and wasps, cloud-pricked
Canada Geese, chain-linked fence. Now climb
into Indiana, beloved corn fiefdom, to brag
about basketball, to step behind the arc and drain
three-pointers, to quench our thirst at Seven Eleven
with resinous Mountain Dew, preamble
to Seagram's, which we pass around the bonfire
before basement lights dim and we thrash
like captive hawks. Erik, Alan, Nina, Mike,
you grew up so fast, I hardly had a chance to write
about Ohio. I hardly had a chance to savor Shoney's
buffet and Red Lobster butter. Goodbye, friends.
May you find your voice in the emerging global economy.
Goodbye, I-75. May the deer that line your shoulders
grow wings. Goodbye, two A.M. stars romancing
Rust Belt cities, backyard tents, public parks,
I have breathed your night air, sweated your Augusts,
biked your pitted streets. When I return, I will
climb your Ziggurats. I will wait in line with my children
at the base of Sears (now Willis) Tower
and tell them stories about growing up,
this tower, then, the tallest in the world.

Concrete Laundromat

You don't know it yet, but today
you will open a hole in your head
the size of two quarters,
and your mother will see the savage white
eye of your skull. Won't that be an ugly
thing to behold on a Saturday morning.

Someday she will tell you how she felt
she must collect every drop of blood
poured from your head. She will say
a stranger carried you to his car
while she pressed clean shirts
against your wound. She remembers

shirts soaked red, still warm
from the dryer. She forgets
the stranger's name. What seems
real: scar, white eye closed below
the seam, those fragile hours
stitched in the retelling.

Black Jack Peers Over the Bed

Fee-fi-fo-fum, I smell the blood…

—Giant

Down below, Jack fathoms
vacant boots wide as trucks,
laces thick as fitness rope
slung from his high school gym.
He snaps pictures with his phone
because this tale just turned
crazy. No one will believe the boots'
totemic gloom without proof.

Warm wind against Jack's throat
as he tries to comprehend their bulk,
so opposite his airy climb,
so anti-bloom, these boots.
He feels flimsy as a daisy
compared to jagged tread,
gaping jaws frozen mid-yawn,
swollen tongues. Rank odor.

Scorched earth and gutted swine

wafting up from empty leather.

Gentle reader, it's not the boots

Jack dreads, but power's feet

for which the boots were built, officer

who shoots twelve times,

would snap his toothpick spine,

pepper-blind his mother's eyes.

Not the boots,

but what the boots imply.

Ann Arbor

Our landlord said we should find a hotel
while he tacked and stained the oak floors,
but we were broke, so Dad pitched a tent
in the backyard beside the great tree,
where my mind climbed among fruit
flies and caterpillars, hungry for cherries
I couldn't reach. Only birds and Mr. Dodge,
our landlord, balanced on his ladder, angling
his silver pole with telescopic extension,
could pluck those rubies I would later
link to Plato tending his fire, Freud,
Marx. He passed a few down,
and we stuffed our mouths and pockets.
At night we lay on foam mats
beneath a single sheet, July's wet heat.
Those blinking hours before sleep,
I assessed the seams, triangular panels
that composed a ceiling, nylon mesh
through which I watched branches bow.
Cherries dropped safe as snow falling
into snow until, by chance, one struck
the tent's taut roof. Mom stirred,

shifted her weight. The unborn child
stuck in breech stomped her bladder.
I remember she unzipped the door,
crawled out like a she-animal, low-slung
middle scraping the tent's under-lip.
She hiked her nightgown, and I heard
water (not blood), smelled rotten fruit,
not the iron tang that would linger state
to state—doctors' bills, late fees—at least
he's alive, they said. A miracle to wake
early and hear his voice, brother born
blue who needs a little money.
He's looking for an apartment.
His girlfriend carries a baby.

Self-Portrait with Silly Putty

Charlie Brown must be the one who suffers.

—Charles Schulz

I didn't laugh while pinching Silly Putty
between my thumb and forefinger,
flattening space-age flesh into a disk.

With all the seriousness of a bench scientist
working late, I pressed the comics page,
extracting Charlie's face. I stretched

beyond limits of legibility, Charlie Brown
thin and translucent, like a small window
with a peach-colored shade.

And seeing he could stretch no further,
I folded his face in my palm,
kneading—what was it

about the boy I wanted to contort?
The expression of defeat,
each loss I knew I could not erase

I transformed into a rocket

before rolling a perfect sphere,

a better world that bounced.

One Lousy Enemy

I'm thinking of the quiet Milwaukee street
where a skinhead knocked me off my bike.
This is not a loss too great to understand.
Not like losing a country or the will to speak.
Just a bike. Chrome frame, gooseneck, spokes.
Another theft in some American outpost,
another boy left flat on his back, blinking
at the sky, listening to his chain *click, click*
goodbye. I'm thinking about the difference
between that boy, age nine, and me
riding to work, pant cuffs stuffed in socks,
wind scraping my eyes to tears, so many tears
one might guess the girl I love is buried
in the cemetery I pedal near. But I'm not crying.
I'm thinking how lucky to live here now
and not Jerusalem during Crusades, or Odessa
with its pogroms, or Gulf Port with its slaves.
I'm thinking about my sloppy childhood,
preoccupied with BMX and rock music,
those gaping Sunday streets where I could ride
to hell and back with Jews, Muslims, and atheists,
our tee shirts taut sails, our callused palms

and checkered Vans, thighs pumping uphill,

elbow to elbow, free-born, well-fed children, rolling

past the mall like a glittering train, between our legs

bikes with sexy names like Redline, Haro, Hutch.

Especially Hutch. If ever asked to lie naked

with a bike for Annie Leibovitz, it will be a Hutch

I clutch. I'm putting romance into perspective,

beginning with my love of bikes, for which I am

not ashamed. We boys built ramps that sent riders

skyward in perpetuity, the big blue catching me

like a pop fly or a Tom Cruise or whatever I aspired

to be. This is what it felt like to ride and jump

a bike in 1986, Milwaukee, and this is how it feels

to look back on my stunned self, sickle-armed

off my seat by a shirtless teenage prick. How it feels

to put loss into perspective, as a lucky man should,

when thinking about stolen bikes and skinned knees

and one lousy enemy, unworthy of history.

Swamp

Where we packed our lips with Skoal,
spread Miss March across our wobbly lust.
Her hobby, "surfing," fairytaled in Santa Monica,
where boys like us could not exist. Storm blown
boys swaddled in camouflage, rifles cocked,
pellets thwapping plastic cups. Boys plagued
by eczema, cysts, and baby fat. Tadpole boys.
Bloodroot boys. Pressure-cooked platefuls of us
with nothing to do but sweat and kill croakers
until dark, until the butchering sun quit
and we tightroped a steel rail home.
By God, sometimes the iron trestle shook
and we flopped into a ditch. The L&N passed,
that giant, one-eyed snake—yellow, red,
black boxcars filled with alien freight.
The moon too far to shoot, we hopped
a split rail fence into the Holstein pasture
and finally the Dollar General parking lot,
where, slumped as sacks of flour, we vowed
we'd be soldiers. We'd die together.

Narcissus and Narcissus

This white and yellow bloom
poses on a slender, hairless stem.

His membranous tunic opens
to the sun, his eye

reflects in a clear spring,
youth's dreamhaze looking back.

He has six sides, a natural geometry.
A damp, sticky surface.

His voice tuned by a slight
tension. Take away his clothes

and his naked body conveys
vitality, a quavering excitement.

The tapering arms, pale skin
escape classification.

Light shines on his sharp-cut chin.

How old would you say?

Certainly younger than me,
with that ardent body, still

in love with that ardent body.

The Heroic Age

After photographs by Herbert Ponting

These images of windswept ice could be
a physical expression of adversity,
but I'm searching for something else
in this record of unmapped routes, scrolled
auroras, heavy sledges pulled by men
low on food, stubborn men photographed
smoking pipes in snug winter quarters,
spiked sealskin boots stowed beneath
wooden bunks, ropes rafter-hung,
sagbellied socks, a box of Fry's Malted Cocoa.

They will reach the South Pole in second place,
33 days after Amundsen, then perish
on the return journey. Does it matter
how slowly one freezes
if one fails to reach the South Pole first?
As with so much, the prize changes
over time: fabled sea route passes through
El Dorado, ripples into Terra Nova,
where marooned explorers visible
in an expedition atlas await spring,

29

the playful certainty in their unmoving

eyes—maybe what I'm after.

Welcome, Dangerous Life

The doctors guessed your guts were snarled,
so they strapped you to a board,

inched a hose down your esophagus,
pumped you full of X-ray dye.

Now shuffle close, play peek-a-boo
behind your mother's thigh.

Hello. Goodbye. Son, there's more.
I'll shape that room before its memory dims,

white-blue walls, wires up your arm,
skin still downy from the womb.

Nurses take you out and there we sit,
stewed in antiseptic air. A wheeled IV

squeaks, sour smell of grief, our minds
buttoned to your body down the hall,

where they shield your infant head

behind lead plates, the X-ray's eye

getting at the truth about your bowels.
We know it's for the best,

doctors doing this detective work
like archeologists freeing frescos

sealed by plaster. No, not like that.
You'll learn I rush comparisons.

This night is *like* nothing.
Two people on a foldout bed,

one gave birth ten hours past,
the other pleads.

Burning the Nest

Earlier I watched wasps prick the air,
glide between sunflower and nest—gray bulb,
featureless as a cloud except for the black,
operatic mouth frozen in a silent cadenza.

Now they sleep inside their paper hub,
capsuled for the night, and I cross the lawn
bundled in raincoat, winter scarf, leather gloves,
sweating hard as I wrap the nest in garbage bags
that stipple like a fresh tar glaze.

My children look out from a square pocket of light,
behold how the nest draws the match's heat,
how fire furrows from plastic to paper,
a few fleet wasps suspended in daggering light.

Orange flakes flutter to ash, then the whole wasp-head
whooshes in blankets of flames. In the Garden of Love
you cannot relax, Rumi says. Nor in the Garden of Loss,
nor in raincoat, nor scarf, nor gloves. Die now,
I say. Die now in this love.

II. Love Debt

Rhapsody for Real Estate

Reel me house to house,
our bank account ready for its root canal. *good metaphor*
Let's wander mid-century moderns,
poor cousins of Frank Lloyd Wright,
who flunked geometry because their flat-tops
failed to shed water. We can pitch
a new roof, replace this wine-stained carpet
with hardwood. Maybe walnut,
maybe oak—either way, I'll whack
those planks into place. You can cook,
I can clean. Picture me on my knees
scrubbing toilets beyond innocent. Sweeping
closets. How pretty your dresses will look
chest to back, wife to wife. How sleek
my suits about to board first class
to nowhere. Let's step outside
through sliding doors: O emerald square!
O butter-haired willow where a tire swing
drops like a hypnotist's watch. We're ready
to sway in hammocks, eavesdrop on katydids
as Jefferson did while framing our pursuit.
Let's hold hands and float like Wendy

and Peter from backyard to half-bath
to master bath, unafraid of headache, allergy,
gas—our tiny tribes of medicine will colonize
these cabinets. My bride, our future
draws light and shadow through these blinds,
the yin and yang of dusk, and then the need
for bedside lamps, for we must read Tolstoy
aloud before sleep, before conception,
before track lights twist their little necks
to brighten our wild-haired infant.
I write this poem for him or her, for you, for we
should have a home where time hammers us
into place, all of us safe beside eternal
spice rack and knife block, apart from cracked
cement and crippled hula hoop, a home
where we see ourselves reflected in polished granite
countertops, midnight black, eyes within the rock.
Or, if not a home, at least this poem where we walk
barefoot across hardwood, whispering walnut, walnut, walnut.

Interview

A man holds out his hand,
says, "Nice suit."
I am not in the mood to lie. I will fly
back to Michigan without a job.
Here is a man without a job
who wears a filthy Lakers tee-shirt.
Can't name a single lake in L.A.,
then I remember Minnesota lost
its team, but the name stuck:
"Land of 10,000 Lakes"
transplanted in California sand,
a global brand. No incentive to amend
the name to something that makes sense:
L.A. Headshots, L.A. Big Ones. Haha.
He wants a dollar. Shooting for
$80,000 a year. "Nice suit"
hangs in the air, his open palm
an extension of the interview,
one last trick question. I think,
Okay, a dollar. Reach for
wallet—empty pocket.
Forget hand, Lakers—how

will I fly home without I.D.?
I have nothing, I say,
and it's true. I can tell by his face
he thinks I'm full of $hit. New suit.
New shoes—never worn
such shine—chewing up my heels.
"Just a dollar, man." As if
I'm doing this for him,
opening my briefcase at his feet,
rummaging through resumes,
work samples. Eighty bucks in cash,
MasterCard, Visa Gold—Lord knows
how much I've lost, how much
he thinks I'll offer.

Husband, Mugged

Rather than discuss the pain,
I prefer to explain how anything,
in a certain light, appears inspired,
and to prove it I crease the mugging
like origami and set it before my wife,
such that she might appreciate the swirling
white swans I glimpsed while being stomped
and the monkey-shaped bruise climbing my ribcage.

I suggest the beating began up-tempo,
a bassist's big hands plunking out blows,
cymbals ringing as my coins sprinkled the asphalt.
I add trumpet and sax,
a flatted-fifth played *adagio*,
a keyboard's dark-timbered solo
entering when I cupped my left eye and fell
sideways, off the curb, into the street.

I know very little about dance but I imagine
two dancers, curled like children,
tumbling the narrow tunnel of my consciousness.
And I describe their slow, synchronized rising

41

as the yellow stage lights dim and a hollow
organ fills the auditorium with my yearning
to remain material, to be nailed to the stony earth
like a granite monument.

I don't tell her I felt indefinite afterwards,
as if painted in a downpour, a background figure
staggering toward the subway steps,
onto the train, back to my hotel room,
where I rewound the tape to see if, in fact,
a set-designer erected those storefronts,
poured my coffee, placed two men behind me
and wrapped the whole scene in darkness.

Floating Exhibit

Questions remain about Bronze-Age
clans who trolled the Euphrates
and converted palm-sized shells
into razors. One kneeled to shave

beside a spring or puddle filled
by fresh swales off the delta. Here's
the evidence: baked in clay—kneeling
male, sixth millennium B.C.E.,

oyster blade, ceramic dish, oily obsidian
wedge that broke black silt on the rich
alluvial plain three thousand years before
"alluvium" sifted from a Latin stream.

Imagine plows teaching oxen to bow,
the agricultural boom—surplus sheep,
slaughter pens, wheat sealed from flies,
stowed in pots, the same clay carved

into tokens by accountants who concurred—
we must denote the difference between one

and ten sheep, more wool and meat
for kings, for scribes, for Enheduanna,

priestess of the moon, who sharpened
her reed stylus, scored the world's first
poems. Study what happens behind
the glass: a statuette, naked, striped

with brown paint, folds his arms
around his chest. Appraise the smooth,
clay head, imperious face, or is it grief,
stranger? I can't decide

what residue of self we share. Here,
in a museum, where glossy fliers
advertise origin as "a common kiln,"
we curious children and children all

grown up, look back through proto-
cuneiform, beveled mugs, toward Uruk,
breeding ground for knowledge,
obscure moniker. Starbucks

open for business outside a glazed
window. Traffic stops and goes.

The Euphrates flickers through
the reeds, right on schedule. Outside,

a blue-green sky. It's very quiet
here. The air smells like polymers
and rubble.

Prodigal Self

Part of me wriggles free,
catches an updraft and turns
unmercifully into a man who spits,
clambers on a bus, says, "Goddamn,
I am not afraid of my humanity."

Oh, everyone, forgive that fucker
who thinks he invented fire
while singing in the shower,

the self who wanders
Manhattan like a panting phantom.
In the background, two lamps
wired for love, one crooked
spoke of lightning.

Forgive his rum-splattered hair,
his unexcused absence,
shipwrecked glare,

his search for grandeur in a tavern mirror,
Henry-keen hunger,

tiger-deep stare
targeting women who smile
over chardonnay, blackened salmon.

Forgive his hunger,
happening again, filling him
like a soap bubble large enough to contain all belligerence and blasphemy.

Where? At what hour will he land?
Poor self, fragile as a cherry blossom,
finally ready to sleep
in the wide lap of Father's mercy.
He could arrive any moment,

thinks part of me who never left.
The good son who fattens a calf
slaughters his resentment.

No Emergency

The twins—one perfect replica of the other—
slept in another room. They ruined her

body, she said, lifting her shirt, folding
the waistband down an inch, so I could see

her scar's cautious smile, plum stretch
marks. The twins—one plea, one whimper—

stirred. In that room, no way to tell
what would repel, what would attract.

I watched her untie her braid, pull her hair
straight. The wine rose to my head.

"Sit close to me," she said. And I knew
this would be a poem where I moved

away instead, where I looked down
at a sword of sunlight on the carpet,

heard the wail of an ambulance

kill a short silence. Why change

the facts? No one will ever know
unless I describe sirens laying

equal claim to public and private,
the red we shared, a touch to the leg,

kiss to the forehead. How we woke
in a cage and howled like wolves.

Incredible Shrinking Man

His jacket is bright blue and swallows him
like a balloon. His head an apple, now
plum, now seed of a grape. His screams,
inchoate whistles, fade beneath
The Albatross Diner's afternoon rush:
orders from cooks, pots and pans,
waitresses with their giant steps.
What's that you say, little man?
Your body is less than a pea,
and soon you'll ride
the backs of
dust mites

.

Just a speck now, a point on a line,
imaginary to everyone but mathematicians
and schizophrenics. Before I go, I do
something very cruel. I brush crumbs
from the counter and finish his soup.
The crumbs look like asteroids, I'm sure.
The soup must be unfathomable.

When his wife returns, I take his clothes
and pay his bill. Holding out enormous hands,
knowing she will weep, I take her too
and tell her everything. It's the same story.
I tell her the same story.

We Played Them Fast and Made Mistakes

All those breakneck bluegrass tunes, "Devil's Dream,"
"Fire on the Mountain," "The Girl I Left Behind"—
souped-up testaments to loneliness, ill will,
and reckless love. How difficult it was to take it
note by note, resolve your alto with my baritone,
harmonize the double-stops. Mozart said composing
was effortless as drinking water. Mozart was a prodigy.
For us, a simple, happy tune, when rushed, falls flat
or pitches sharp as tragedy. One must pause,
admit defeat, start from scratch. No first place.
Rest.
Slower, Love.
We patient are the blessed.

Morning, Children

One wakes with earache,
another screams milk.

A never-to-be

slips under our sheets,
part wedge, part bridge.

Failed Still Life with Jealousy

The man beside the woman,
three buttons of his shirt open,

hand raised to brush a crumb
from her chin. Lips paused

to draft a kiss. Fingers
ready to receive her fingers

ready to receive the cigarette
he'll pass like a sacrament.

I want eyes that follow
the same smooth flight,

a tongue that shares the same
burnt taste. Sun breaks

beneath a cloud. Their hands braid.
Can't stop this movement

nor infinite permutations of light

on her shoulder. Bare skin

shrugged from shyness,
green's sweet redness.

Confessional

I loved a woman who loved cats
more than people. Pet his back.
Let him lick your face, she said.

I did because who knows
what might have happened
if I did not.

That cat killed everything.
I saw him pounce and release
a chipmunk. Pounce.

Release. Until chipmunk stopped
moving. Then anger slapped me,
and I hissed. Why

write poems unless
you can express
such ruin gratefully?

Inversions

One day, instead of thinking,
Late for work,
we think, *Into the room a unicorn will run.*

Cradle stuffed with fruit.
Coffin lined with books.
Flipped has the reservoir of everyday thought.

Our gladioli upside down,
petals pinwheeling underground
while roots claw toward the winter moon.

High, massive clouds drop
to drowse as dew
on the smooth brow of a cactus.

And we too are tempted
to convert during these strange storms,
tip the old reservoir,

such that I might marry a painter
and you a chef,

our children slumped on strangers' laps.

We could easily slip across the ocean,
slide our tongues
into Greek or Icelandic and ride freely

that dangerous white mount
who draws figure eights around our heads
with a sleek, opalescent horn.

Forgiving Indianapolis

I would like to sit with you at Velocity Bar
once your shift is up, Veronica,
once you have removed your name
from your lapel and hung your Marriott blazer
in the employees-only closet. We can laugh
and forgive Indianapolis for snow in April.
We can forgive tall girls blown in
from coasts, their volleyball bags
and matching sweat suits filling the lobby.
Forgive volleyball. Forgive the website
where my reservation has slipped
through a wormhole into another universe.
Forgive the other universe. Veronica, my muse
of available rooms, walk me down
the counter to a working computer and whisper
how sorry, how truly sorry. Forgive
tall fathers who have come to watch
tall daughters morph into windmills.
Forgive these girls, for they deserve
a good night's sleep in queen-sized beds
before the tournament. Forgive Hilton, Hyatt,
and all downtown Indianapolis for filling up.

Forgive my layover and late arrival, blue

economy-class blankets and the task

of luggage. Forgive the corny names

of hotel bars, beery winds and 80's playlists.

Wake me up before you go-go,

Veronica, it's almost midnight and I'm hanging on

like a yo-yo. Forgive overhead speakers

and solo piano colliding with Wham, as I forgive

you, Veronica, for wanting to send me away,

for frown and consternation, for the end

of conversation. A cab waits

to take me to a distant Marriott,

fifty dollars from downtown,

where I will lie in the dark,

imagining how love feels

in another universe.

Self-Portrait as a Mole at the End of the World

I say "hawk" when asked by our children
what animal I would choose, except nights
I fear the end is near, news of chlorine gas,
missile tests, drone attacks. Those nights
I pick a mole because something soft

and harmless should survive a holocaust,
even if it means shrinking to one-fiftieth my size
and hiding underground until clouds drain
their poison and the great fires hiccup smoke
and the champion virus dulls its sword.

When sweetening roots signal a safer world,
I'll surface, break through bone mounds
to sniff out grace. Nearly blind, I will not see
our crumbling, ant-lacquered street, blue,
luminous dragonflies haloing the porch.

I'll snuffle through dust, pink feet padding
home, where I'll rake my harmless claws
upon the mat and cast my small shadow on the bathroom
floor—the cold, white tiles still intact, shower cap

hanging like a dry mushroom on the brass knob.

I'll recall, with my genius snout, Sunday morning
long ago, lavender soap, comb pulled behind
your ear, parting hair for which I hunt,
the old world still wet in my mind, like a robe
that draped your shoulders once.

1-800-FLOWERS.COM

Cut cleanly because you're meant to forget
missing roots once shipped nitrogen

to paint the gaudy heights. Woozy tulips
tilt toward the window like history

tilts toward the present anniversary,
but just as easily they decorate birthday,

wake, or baby shower. Red, white, yellow
roses stunned and stunning—Miss New Jersey

mailed to Miss Missouri—at any hour,
for any occasion, to complement *I love you.*

I'm sorry. Godspeed,
my brief and rootless beauty.

III. Restless Animal

Reseeding a Nature Trope

Notice what happens when you plant the idea,
Mother Earth, with its custody of baby's breath,
cougar silence, sucking mud, and spores.

No parish priest, no heavenly reward.
Forget climate data for the moment.
Forget the Enlightenment. Focus on

cattails roughing up a little breeze,
hill-cupped sky, light-soaked leaves,
purple stamens dabbed with pollen.

You might spiral hawks forward
or curve back to hawks hovering
within the gray fog of childhood.

Stalk a ripple of deer. Skim
mountain lakes with ice-edged dawn.
Spell it out with sunlight. Scurry

squirrels limb to sill. Ash the night
with bats. Notice how the idea swells

hemisphere to habitat, seeding margins,

scaling hollows, jagging slopes,
surf and marsh, where flocks erupt
and fling outward, sifting past Orion

like interstellar dust. Speech
fills the central figure, *Mother
Earth*, like a pit, like a moth inside

moon-white silk, or a boy awash the green
stream's plush. Grip my hand, son,
let's cross a summer lawn, enjoy enduring

connections. Adhere like water within water,
daughter. Can you read "horsefly"?
Can you say "beanvine"?

So many conceptions
feel umbilical as we stretch—word to world—
her two-way tether.

Athena

What do we call an embryo after
a doctor says, *I'm sorry*?

Someone who knows, tell me
what to call matter
that will not bud.

Good and wise, teach me how to multiply,
how to flood the plain.
I want to hear the heart's measured stamp,

hold a notion given shape,
a body wrapped in sunny cloth.

I'm thinking of a girl with ruffled hair.
One toe sweeps the sand.
Her parents read beneath a green umbrella.

My mind constructs their sense of triumph,
their work-proud pleasure,
their birthmark smoothly made,
wonder of wonders sprung from

a tiny-celled thimble.

Her outline vibrates in the sun
like she who split her father's skull,
leaped whole from his pain.

Machine Overheard Teaching Boy to Read

What is in the mitten   click on

the question mark   that's right

a question mark shows what is in the mitten

click on the skunk

down by the words   the mitten

rewritten   go on   practice reading

this page   click on the rewind button

repeat   what is in the mitten

great   now you can play it back

click on *what*   this is not the word

what   click on *what*   that's right

click on *in*   click on *in*

click on   correct   click on *mitten*

this is what sentences should look like

click here   this is not the word mouse

a mouse is in the mitten

which of these words goes in   this

blank   that's right   a mouse is

in the mitten   the sentence should

say a mouse is in the mitten   correct

a porcupine is in the mitten   that's right

a porcupine is in the mitten

you got it   a porcupine

is in the mitten   that's right

the sentence should say

what is in the mitten   the sentence should

say   click here   the sentence should

say   click on the pencil when you are finished

correct   you made a great story.

Morals from *The Treasury of Pleasure Books for Young Children*

> *The sky is falling! The sky is falling!*

> —Chicken Little

On her way to warn the king,
Chick meets Rooster, Goose, Duck,
and Fox—who tricks the birds,
gobbles them up. Or not.
Sometimes the flock escapes.
Versions of this tale go back
twenty-five centuries, I'm told.
All mock mass hysteria,
but the moral hangs on king's reply:
Don't believe everything you're told, child.
Never lose sight of real danger.
Have courage!

When wind shakes the oak
and acorns augur wicked weather,
don't tremble, child. Storms rinse
the mudhole past, tip ships,
spill empire with a sneeze.
Ask the three little priests

about churches flying off
foundations, the Reformation,
Voltaire in prison, natural selection—
Darwin storming the Galapagos,
his gale inside a hollow quill.
Don't believe everything you read,
child. Aristotle wrote, "What is a nut
if not a tree in the end?" In the end,
every story finds a purpose. So
the story goes. If Chick was destined to feel
sky fall on her bald head, if Fox evolved
to eat chicken, if what survives spreads—
how good the goods?
How fine the soul's merchandise?
In other words, my twenty-first century
chirp, who knows?
The king is dead.
The sky may or may not be.
Brace thyself.

Closed KFC

No one sings for the franchise, nor for the glistening
forehead above the register. The air motionless

and heavy. The odor of skin does not ring a plastic
fork. No one stands behind you. The bird that died

last year will not cross the city in your teeth. Where
biscuits rose noiselessly out of brown froth. Where

prairie-breast hunger bridged the freeway between
strangers. Go, friend, find fresh salt for your animal

soul. And after the longing ensues, raise your wing
before the multitude. Strip the bones. Swallow everything.

Scout

Bees in search of home kaleidoscope condos
where cherry blossoms bloomed last year. New York
changed and bees stayed bees—the same old *swell*
or *knot* or *static eye*, whatever words I might have used
in last year's poem. Bees, like refugees, adapt,
send scouts who search real estate alone.
Alone, without collective sight, some lose
their sense, careen windshields, landfills, mistake
McDonald's signs for dandelions. So many ways
bees die. But some survive, fly Central Park,
find hidden honeysuckle woods, knowing nectar
must be found before the hive will move. Mountain aster,
buttercup, any blossom worthy of cartography,
they body-map in loops and points and semicircle flights—
motifs for luring distant minds and wings
that blur and chime domestically like blessings.

Trapped American Goldfinch

How long must I watch him strobe
the ceiling of my garage
like the wild eye of a child's flashlight?

Shouldn't he be flitting an aspen grove
or throwing his lemon-bright stitchery
against a white stucco church?

Can't he see the clouds and hear the trills,
sense the junipers shoulder up
to dusk, bees sizzling round the porch?

And doesn't he have a song for dusk,
spreading overhead like a slate terrace,
smudging out the day's raggy shadows?

Is he waiting for the sun to belly under
so he can fine-tune
a preamble to the knuckling rain?

Surely the moon will call him out
once the sky darkens and stretches

its gloom-rich resin.

Then again, he may seek
more than relief from heat,
something splendid and articulate,

like an albatross tilting toward Alaska,
lulling the wind with Emersonian
lectures on the life long-lifted.

Or has he come to remind me
that among these practical American tools
a restless animal forever circulates,

circulates inside this two-car garage,
my mind tethered to the tight,
two-car circumference of his flight?

As long as we're bound, shouldn't we float
like breeze-bounced spores
or find a fence to jackknife?

Might we drizzle down the Delaware,
unreel our wooings by that water,
beside those throaty steel mills?

An old owl splashes his pinions there
and claims the whole country
once sparkled like Jerusalem,

every leaf tremble, every bus and beggar,
every millstoned thought of a new world
once hot as an oil drum campfire.

Are you the pilgrim I would be,
searching for seeds, breadcrumbs, dew drops,
if not for this sensible garage?

Fleeting shadow on the cinderblock wall
who twines my vision with a strangled
frenzy of wings, go now. Take me with you.

Night Terrors

Strange that starving grizzlies eat their young
while nature (culture?) programmed me to share,
sacrifice, lose sleep—snap awake, stagger
through the hall at two A.M., rehearsing songs
fathers everywhere, back to who knows
when, sing, night after night. Hear her
wheeze. Watch her chest rise. Why fear?
Blackout shades blunt dawn, nightlights show
she's fine. Still, the drive to save her life,
calm her infant cries—*Beware!*
Some suffocate. Some you can't revive.
Our best defense this pure, intoxicating fear,
distilled, drip-by-drip, through blood-choked time,
the cries not hers alone but mine, fierce and older.

Twin Days

"Largest Annual Gathering of Twins in the World"

—Guinness Book of World Records

There and they're—a pigtailed pair
who share the same vulnerability

to glaucoma. Two more match
tie-dyed shirts, Kruse Brothers

Car Club hats. Duplicate nails,
diapers, flip-flops—thousands

converge in Twinsberg, Ohio
every August. In Twinsberg, Ohio,

the FBI scan irises, freckles,
overbite, even advanced facial

recognition software fooled
by small changes in lighting.

Scientists, too, pitch white tents,

ask Rob and Ron to sip juice

from tiny cups. How's it taste?
How's it taste? Thanks to twins,

they calculate height at 80%
heritable, IQ at 75%. Perhaps

too alike, too like eugenics—
eugenical, I think. Reading now

about two couples raising identicals
200 miles apart. Mothers say both

took first steps March 8, same
lazy eye, same mean streak.

What Fernando Saw

As we drive home from Daisy Scouts
you tell me you are scared—
during school Fernando peeked
under Emma's hat and saw no hair.

The story hurls me out of traffic
and into the wilderness
you navigate, vines of dread
slung over Emma's smooth scalp.

You can't peek beneath the skin
nor delve where cells replicate
their logic, diacope of nuclei,
yellowing interior. Ten years

from now, maybe you'll discover
the Latinate labels and ruby
musculature of those ageless models
who pose in high school biology books,

perhaps puzzle out *mutagenesis*
in college, your red hair spilling

over diagrams as you wonder if,

like me, you're wired for melanoma.

The world is safe, I say,

which is somewhat true considering

we ease into a sturdy garage, enough light,

for now, to dodge the errant rake,

                              find the concrete step.

Desolation Canyon

I didn't understand how to erase
our city until I heard the murmuring
melt and stepped out to find a river's
tan felt pinched between red cliffs,
our buildings stripped of windows
and electricity. Who needs dynamite,
two-ton wrecking balls, or hydraulic
shears to collapse the worn out
commercial district. I have this demon
blue sky, stiff wind, undammed water,
a hundred million years of rock.
Who needs mildewing tablecloth,
screech of a wheel, scuffed linoleum,
when I have this morning skyline
quilted in light, convincing me
I behold the last wild place—lie
I collect inside a camera for you, friend,
a panorama of stubborn pretending.

Pando

The world's largest organism is dying.

Some say new growth could save this silver-green
rootstalk topped by quaking, shield-shape leaves—
gust struck, they drop and plate the slope. Skin
soft enough to carve with a dull key
or pocket knife as JOHNNY '12 has done
near other bark-scarred names. Google it:
you'll learn the aspen share a knotted heart.
The Latin translates as "I spread." Scroll down.
You'll notice Pando makes poor firewood but fine
paper, first-rate saunas, where JOHNNY '12
can sweat near KYLE '01—strangers loined
by small, white towels at a luxury hotel.
Cracks along the grain, disease. TRUMP
engraved on rotten trunks. Also, ~~TRUMP.~~

Self-Portrait with Lopper

Today the Tree of Knowledge droops:
too much fruit, too many facts.
Not even nine o'clock and already I want to prune
expert pronouncements with my lopper, which casts
a raptor-beaked shadow on the garden.

And when I lop, I do not discriminate among branches:
anthropology, pure and applied math, particle physics, psychodynamics—
everything psychologists dream about dreaming I lop
as decisively as the subtle knowledge stored
on the thumb of my son who, moments ago, learned how to snap.

How history shudders as I cinch
titanium blades around smooth limbs of the law,
all those plump abstractions dropping like apples
to be hollowed out by bees, bees creeping
out of each edict's pillow-soft core.

And I will continue lopping until I stand shin-deep
in ancient knowledge—Egyptian fractions and Platonic solids
snagging my socks as I shred the old order like Shiva,

making room for a wild radiance

whose name I've forgotten.

Portrait of Utility

Poles point dully at the sky,
rigid, unable to relax
into watercolor or panoramic photograph

because of the power they manage,
like executives in brown suits
declining to set down briefcases.

I don't feel compelled to climb them
as I might an apple tree because they reek
creosote, splinters villainous,

but I still applaud their fellowship
when, arm in arm, they stand
against prairie tornado or delta flood,

reminders of interdependence,
old, flat-footed Bolsheviks
under lofty satellite chatter,

under space and stars beyond stars,
from ice-chipped dawn to warm summer darkness,

asserting their humble logic

on the landscape like a stiff infantry
standing soot-wet in the rain,
awaiting orders unknown to birds

who settle down like notes on a staff
or squirrels who tightrope the slack,
tails —?—?—?—like that.

Audubon Exit

Was once, too, at the full, and round earth's shore.

—Matthew Arnold

Our guide says new moon tides transform
that little copse into an island, tells of finding
sharks' teeth, sea stars, and this—from her
burlap pack she pulls a turtle shell, passes it
so we can thumb pale barnacles
locked against the shell's humped keel.
I want to know more about this shell,
those gulls who glide and plunge above
the gray Atlantic shelf, the seal who bobs
like a black buoy. What type of algae
banks red against the sandbar's edge?
Then the sun drops behind a cloud,
and the sea, having lost its sequins, becomes
a field of slate. I feel I should escape
all prior knowledge, wander shore, turning
shells over in my hand, deciding for myself
why we're whorled and thinned by time,
strewn across the beach like pieces
of a shattered clock. Soon I'll wander

from my body and my body's guide, read
scrolls of white foam, listen to the hollow
conch laugh, and laugh with God
at God's joke.

IV. Less-than-perfect chain

Thanatos and Eros

From my window, boys with guns
close in around my neighbor's son,
who is out of rounds. Tulips
                    find
a front row seat, and in the upper deck
a circling hawk carves a noose
in onion-skinned noon. The boys' game
circles
too—a loop of shoot, fall, rise
to shoot and fall again. My graveyard
gaze funnels. I won't play, instead
                    notice
more delicate reminders of death,
this desk lamp, whose clear
glass waist holds a dry bouquet
brown
and white petals that look alive
when I tug a little brass chain. *Click.*
And just like that the window
                    flaunts
two women who rent the house next door,
allowing them to claim a dainty patch of grass

no larger than a parking space, spread

towels

on the lawn, strip to bathing suits. Still

winter-white, their legs enter like

meteors, strike the game's axis

> alter

its gravitational constant. The boys stop

as if halted by the whistle of a referee.

Time-out for them to scoop pleasure

dollops

from bodies warmed by the sun

that warmed Plato as he measured men

against gods and found the difference

> slim

enough to overcome with a definition of Eros

void of lust, which his pupils forgot

as they raced down the Athenian hill,

past

olive groves and date palms, beyond

shrines to muses, sticks in hand.

Tagged

in a photo uploaded to Facebook.
How happy I look
grilling with Mike—bald man to my right
who never finished his thesis
on Crane. Madness and sorrow
tagged him for so many years.

Abandoned gear: Labatt Blue,
Mike's perfectly smooth head,
crescent eyes, greased teeth,
burnt bratwurst. Smoke tags
the humid dusk, kids play
the same game we played in the park.

Remember trying to catch fast someone
who disappeared? I wanted that
dandelion necklace, so I chased her
over blacktop, gravel. She juked
into shadow before I could scream,
You're it. In the slippery present,

Mike texts, "slept poorly,"

and I browse yard sales, hunting
good deals in stranger's garage,
touching a Snow White lunchbox
as a psychic might when asked to find
a missing girl. All the while,

my Facebook timeline progresses
toward its concordant whole.
The photo stills a backyard in Ohio,
where lightning bugs pulsed
and frogs chugged, tags one
momentary self, who blinked.

Aftermath

Drunk, barely able to walk, Alan turns the shotgun
on Superior, daughter-killer. Pine and sugar maple
line her shore like escorts bowing for a waltz.
Her water-body dazzles blood on dusk. *person. fixation*
Eyes shut, he shoots and feathers plume
against the drooping sun. A harmless loon
he should have missed, like broken apple, skips
and sinks. Two more shots slap the lake
and he sees her, dead one week, rise in smoke
above the double-barrel. Empty boat that took her out
looks glum, oars locked, limp rope tied to dock.
When the final shell is spent, he drops the gun
and runs the driftwood bank toward her dark
expanse. How quickly cold disarms him.

Breaking Bread

I want to flag you down
though you have left
your light-filled hut,
slid into Anahorish
with your translator's keys
and ingredients for seasoned speech.

I want to fasten your lute string
to my throat, enter your museum
all glittered up with Irish water,
myth, and politics, mimicking
that bendy dialect
that butter sunk under,
sipping that blue cream Sweeney sipped.

Listen, you say, the tall silence
can't block my nimble work.
I'll still get the green rain right.
I'll still come when you can't sleep
to thread a river through your ear,
to settle stones in their sockets,
to smooth down the eyelid of evening.

But what about the lean-lipped men
down-bent by prayer?
What about the bearded foam,
the loam and peat pocketed with bones
and the brooding, never-to-be poems
wrenched from cold clod, each one
ringing with your bronze bell?

Listen, you say, every line I built
to be renewed.

What to Do with Minnesota

What to do with muddy fields in fall
besides study the strange loyalty of geese
as they pass disguised as a necklace

over

all that missing corn, the last beets
guarding their sweet magenta. You feel
sorry for the bees, also for yourself
because
you know this isn't March. Remember
when you weren't sure what to do
with muddy fields last

March

and like a beet buried yourself
in memory, the strange loyalty of geese
disguised as seeds blown over earth, all
pasts
planted in the present like new grass
curtained by rain. Forget prophetic
leaves, hard wind, torn.

Body Art

His tattoos want what he wants: wife, daughter,
mother, shower (in that order). Then Lazy Boy, beer,
backyard radio, "Mercy, Mercy Me," baby
drool, shoulder bare. The dagger-staved
skull and scorpion have nothing left
to fear—hospitals are safe. Hands safe.
Head safe. Lungs and heart and balls are safe.
Safe lists lure sleep better than a sheep-count
(sometimes sheep detonate). When he wakes
the ghost-foot-ache annuls his list.
He sees one boot posted upright in the desert,
half in search of other half. His lost
tattoo—orange fish that swam his calf—looks permanent.
His boot, imagined whole, looks innocent.

At the Window

enough draft between

      glass and warped vinyl

frame you taste cold

      air on your lips outside

the quiet climb

      crows smoke your eyes

scale the same dry vine

      how easily you rise

into that elegiac sky

      with a mind as light-

baffling steam

don't be surprised

if you're still

inches from the glass

gray stain on your shirt

garnish of lettuce hanging

off your second button

older now and you know

how long a window lasts

how much renewal costs

how a draft enters

the body leaves

a thrashing noise

Escape from Heroic Music

You can't shake the conductor,
perched like a sunbird, his wand
feeding the universe order and precision,

nor competition for First Chair,
nor musicians seated in rows,
black dresses and tuxedos so alike,

like notes in Europe's vast repertoire—
Bach, Beethoven, Mozart, also unknown
composers who lived long ago, unfinished

scherzos in their head. You can't escape
the tympani's blast, nor the piccolo
who cries in the arms of a viola, *personification*

sounds like Vienna, 1945. Wagner's coda.
You who sailed to another continent,
ears washed out by wind, *linguistic invention*

who stood on a salt-skimmed deck,
a hollow reed, fearing

drums and brass, groan of strings,

the drone of a bassoon
unresolved in the lowest register.

Hoedown for Dualists

Just separate body and soul
into square dance lines and watch yourself
do-si-do down the aisle. Body to the right,
soul to the left, The Great Barn of Being
bitter-sweet with sawdust and manure.
Sway, soul. Sashay, body, so delicious
with pheromones and DNA.
Raise the dead who lie in the hay.
Witness a lamb grazing on weeds
beneath The Great Barn's roof. Pray:
Lord, protect us from rain. There's old Lazarus
staring down at his gray bicep.
There's old Li Po tipping back
his jug of wine, thinking, *What a big dream,*
this life in the world. Pray: Lord,
let me learn the step, and let me pass
without breaking somebody's nose.
Calling out more do-si-dos.
Ace of diamonds, jack of spades,
meet your partner, promenade.
And a body acts on instinct,
and a soul throws amber light

upon your lips and spine.

A swift revolution, this living-dying

day after day, less-than-perfect chain.

All join hands, circle to the south,

put some moonshine in your mouth.

And a tongue sneaks out of its sweat lodge

for a sip, and the Caller calls,

Shoot the star! Box the gnat!

Step forward and do a left-face U turn

back under the raised joined hands

as your body walks forward and around

your soul while doing a right-face

U turn back. End facing each other,

your mind in the starting position,

against oblivion.

Breakfall

How will you manage stairs
when your brittle body trembles
like a piece of straw? Some say

               practice

wearing a tool-belt, a backpack.
Fall in heels, some say. Tuck
your head. Round right angles.
No
straight legs.
No arched spine.
Do not hold your breath.

            Consider

the terrain. Some say
keep lights on, remove rugs.
Grass is not the same as gravel

                 even

for the cannonball. Whether
you slip or you're thrown,
you'll want to slap the earth,
disperse that *whoosh*

       flowing from your fingertips.

Rhapsody for an Optimist

All events are linked together in the best of all possible worlds.

—Pangloss

Listen—a sitar
stirs the beeswax moon from its island   *linguistic invention*
roost.
Ravi Shankar plays The Best of
Ravi Shankar. Slender fingers
                    curve
the ragas merge with a wave's
slurry chorus of froth. I ride this
wave,
sleek as a Monterey seal well-
proportioned as an Armani
                    sail,
to the east, yawning prairie,
Kansas City, Boston and New York
lit
toe to crown. By now, most of Europe
awake, Eiffel Tower—*réveille-toi!*—
                    alert,
baguettes cresting all over France.

111

On the same world, lions of Kenya

lope

the savannah and randy pandas

strip bamboo with their teeth.

                                  At last,

the book I write complete.

The woman I love ferried into pleasure.

Bad

news, bad luck—broken necks

and impalements—let them

                                  pass,

these unbest of all possible

thoughts, anxious blips,

blue

lips and blood pressure pills, dry

little pom-poms of shredded bills,

                                  fraud,

foreclosure—*Adieu! Palaam!* Reverse

your brief distemper aboard a gold

self-

driving Tesla. Enjoy the roadtrip

through Death Valley, Kenneth Koch's

                                  astonished

voice calling forth evening breezes,

rooftop vistas, Sirens' long, luxurious kisses.

Vernice Bianca

Luthiers say you can't replicate an 18th century
Stradivarius—maple back and willow blocks
varnished with honey, egg white, gum arabic.
All but done, Stradivari brushed this *vernice*
bianca, careful not to drip the amniotic gloss
Heifetz would polish two hundred years later,
vanishing fingerprints with a silk handkerchief.

I dry with a cotton towel. Heifetz ends *Souvenir*
de Florence ablaze. Even in his final days,
swollen arm be damned, he'd ornament
a simple phrase. My father, alive, no longer pulls
silver dollars from behind my daughter's ear.
He helps stack dishes on shelves until he can't.
Sits at the ebony table, writes: Milk

Bran flakes

Dr.

His list a ladder into the future
balanced against the old house.
If his legs weren't numb, he'd climb,
empty gutters, prepare for winter. Instead,
he rests—we rest together—out back.

My daughter bows something
she wrote. I recognize.

Ben Gunsberg was born in Virginia and grew up in the Midwest. He attended Miami University (OH), the University of Alabama, and the University of Michigan, where he received his PhD in 2012. His poems have appeared in many literary journals, including *Mid-American Review*, *DIAGRAM,* and *Tupelo Quarterly Review*. He is the author of the chapbook *Rhapsodies with Portraits* and has won a Hopwood Award as well prizes from The Utah Division of Arts and Museums. He lives in Logan, Utah, where he teaches English at Utah State University. Visit his website at www.bengunsberg.com.

CPSIA information can be obtained
at www.ICGtesting.com
Printed in the USA
LVHW090303180719
624482LV00001B/10/P